A TRUE BOOK

W9-CNK-856

My United States

South Carolina

BARBARA A. SOMERVILL

Children's Press®
An Imprint of Scholastic Inc.

Content Consultant
James Wolfinger, PhD, Associate Dean and Professor
College of Education, DePaul University, Chicago, Illinois

Library of Congress Cataloging-in-Publication Data

Names: Somervill, Barbara A., author.
Title: South Carolina / by Barbara A. Somervill.
Description: North Mankato, MN : Children's Press, [2018] | Series: A true
 book | Includes bibliographical references and index.
Identifiers: LCCN 2017048066| ISBN 9780531235799 (library binding) | ISBN
 9780531250921 (pbk.)
Subjects: LCSH: South Carolina--Juvenile literature.
Classification: LCC F269.3 .S66 2018 | DDC 975.7--dc23 LC record available at
https://lccn.loc.gov/2017048066

Photographs ©: cover: Nature Picture Library/Alamy Images; back cover bottom: Sean Pavone/iStockphoto; back cover ribbon: AliceLiddelle/Getty Images; 3 top: Jim McMahon/Mapman ®; 3 bottom: Travel Library Limited/Superstock, Inc.; 4 top: Gilles Delacroix/age fotostock; 4 bottom: alslutsky/Shutterstock; 5 top: Jon Lovette/Getty Images; 5 bottom: Cecil Williams/Getty Images; 7 top: Dave Allen Photography/Shutterstock; 7 center top: Stock Connection/Superstock, Inc.; 7 center bottom: Mary Ann Chastain/AP Images; 7 bottom: Sean Pavone/Alamy Images; 8-9: Richard Ellis/Alamy Images; 11: Danita Delimont/Getty Images; 12: National Geographic Creative/Alamy Images; 13: Mic Smith/AP Images; 14: Bill Lea/Dembinsky Photo Associates/ Alamy Images; 15: pchoui/iStockphoto; 16-17: csfotoimages/iStockphoto; 19: Mladen Antonov/Getty Images; 20: Tigatelu/ Dreamstime; 22 left: Atlaspix/Shutterstock; 22 right: Sakda tiew/Shutterstock; 23 top left: Gilles Delacroix/age fotostock; 23 top right: alslutsky/Shutterstock; 23 center left: Vahan Abrahamyan/Shutterstock; 23 center right: matthewo2000/iStockpho- to; 23 bottom left: Sebastian Janicki/Shutterstock; 23 bottom right: Douglas David Seifert/Pantheon/Superstock, Inc.; 24-25: Buyenlarge/Getty Images; 26: The Trustees of the British Museum/Art Resource, NY; 29: IanDagnall Computing/Alamy Images; 30 top left: Hulton Archive/Getty Images; 30 top right: Atlaspix/Shutterstock; 30 bottom: North Wind Picture Archives; 31 top left: Marynag/Dreamstime; 31 top right: Cecil Williams/Getty Images; 31 bottom left: North Wind Picture Archives; 31 bottom right: SC Governors Office/Alamy Images; 32: Cecil Williams/Getty Images; 33: PhotoQuest/Getty Images; 34-35: Julia Lynn Photography/ Spoleto Festival USA; 36: Streeter Lecka/Getty Images; 37: Hilton Head Island Motoring Festival & Councours d'Elegance; 38: John Wollwerth/Shutterstock; 39: Clemson University International Center for Automotive Research; 40 inset: NRedmond/Getty Images; 40 background: PepitoPhotos/iStockphoto; 41: Jon Lovette/Getty Images; 42 top left: North Wind Picture Archives/Alamy Images; 42 top right: Everett Historical/Shutterstock; 42 bottom left: Everett Collection/age fotostock; 42 bottom right: Charles Colon/TSN/Icon SMI 800/Newscom; 43 top left: Woody Marshall/KRT/Newscom; 43 top right: Mike Fanous/Getty Images; 43 center left: Chuck Kennedy/KRT/Newscom; 43 bottom left: Dwong19/Dreamstime; 43 bottom center: Featureflash Photo Agency/ Shutterstock; 43 bottom right: SC Governors Office/Alamy Images; 44 top: Historical/Getty Images; 44 center: Everett Collection; 44 bottom: Tim Gainey/Alamy Images; 45 top left: Michele Oenbrink/Alamy Images; 45 top right: Franck Fotos/Alamy Images; 45 center: Thinkstock; 45 bottom: North Wind Picture Archives.

Maps by Map Hero, Inc.

Scholastic Inc., 557 Broadway, New York, NY 10012

1 2 3 4 5 6 7 8 9 10 R 28 27 26 25 24 23 22 21 20 19

Front cover: Charleston Race Week

Back cover: Myrtle Beach

Welcome to South Carolina

Find the Truth!

Everything you are about to read is true **except** for one of the sentences on this page.

Which one is **TRUE**?

T or F English settlers were the first Europeans to visit South Carolina.

T or F South Carolina fought on the side of the South in the Civil War.

Find the answers in this book.

Key Facts

Capital: Columbia

Estimated population as of 2017: 5,024,369

Nickname: Palmetto State

Biggest cities: Charleston, Columbia, North Charleston

UNITED STATES

South Carolina

Contents

THE **BIG** TRUTH!

Yellow jessamine

What Represents South Carolina?

Eastern tiger swallowtail

Liberty Bridge in Falls Park

3 History

4 Culture

Students march in a civil rights demonstration in 1960.

FREEDOM

5

This Is South Carolina!

TENNESSEE

1

Chattooga River

Caesars Head State Park

Shoeless Joe Jackson Museum and Baseball Library

Chattooga

GREENVILLE

SPARTANBURG

ROCK HILL

Cherokee Path

Piedmont Plateau

NORTH CAROLINA

Sand Hills State Forest

Mann-Simons Cottage

Wateree

Lynches

Pee Dee

N W E S

0
Miles

SOUTH CAROLINA

★ **COLUMBIA**

Columbia State Capitol

Congaree National Park

Lake Marion

Black

Santee

Alligator Adventure

MYRTLE BEACH

G St

Brookgreen Gardens

GEORGIA

Savannah

Edisto

Lake Moultrie

Battery Park

The South Carolina Aquarium

2

3

Intracoastal Waterway

Center for Birds of Prey

Fort Sumter

CHARLESTON

HILTON HEAD BEACH

Sea Islands

Parris Island Museum

ATLANTIC OCEAN

① Caesars Head State Park

With views of scenic waterfalls and rugged mountains, this beautiful park in northwestern South Carolina offers experienced and first-time hikers plenty to see. They can also keep an eye out for peregrine falcons, green salamanders, and black bears.

② The South Carolina Aquarium

Located in Charleston, this aquarium's exhibits include coastal sea turtles, touch tanks, an aviary, and a swamp. There are more than 5,000 animals here. The aquarium's goals are to educate people and help conserve wildlife.

③ Center for Birds of Prey

Scientists care for injured birds of prey, including eagles, falcons, hawks, and vultures, at this facility in Awendaw. Visitors can take a tour and watch the birds soar through the sky.

④ Grand Strand

The Grand Strand is a stretch of sandy beaches in Myrtle Beach. It has water parks, amusement rides, and many other fun things to do. People can see for miles from the top of the giant SkyWheel.

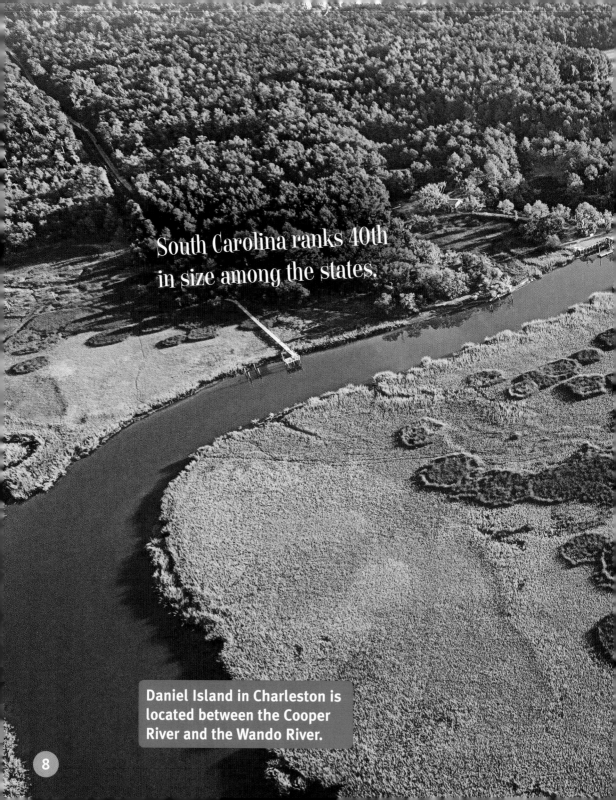

South Carolina ranks 40th
in size among the states.

Daniel Island in Charleston is
located between the Cooper
River and the Wando River.

CHAPTER 1

Land and Wildlife

South Carolina is a small, roughly triangular state in the southeastern United States. Its north side is bordered by North Carolina. Georgia lies to the southwest, while the Atlantic Ocean creates the state's eastern boundary. Between these borders lie sandy beaches, swampy wetlands, and green forests. Rivers stretch across the land, and mountains rise up in the distance. These and other landforms all add up to create a state that is jam-packed with incredible natural scenery.

From the Coast to the Mountains

A broad, flat area called the Atlantic Coastal Plain takes up almost the entire eastern two-thirds of South Carolina. The northwestern area is called the **Piedmont**. The Piedmont is a **plateau** that takes up most of the remaining one-third of the state. It rises up to the Blue Ridge Mountains, which make up a small part of the state on its far northwestern edge. The Blue Ridge Mountains are very old and covered with thick forests.

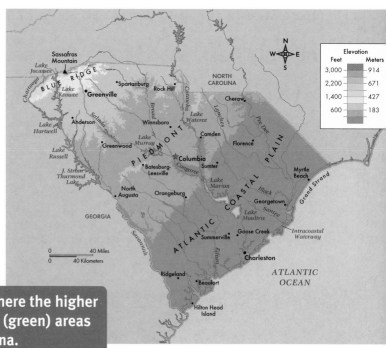

This map shows where the higher (yellow) and lower (green) areas are in South Carolina.

Four Holes Swamp

When people think of swamps, they often picture areas of mucky sludge crawling with bugs. Four Holes Swamp is nothing like that. Located in southeastern South Carolina, it is a flooded forest where 1,000-year-old bald cypress trees rise up from the water. Visitors paddle through the swamp in canoes. They are warned to keep their toes and fingers out of the water. Turtles, alligators, and cottonmouth snakes can all give nasty bites. Bird-watchers can spot herons, ibises, egrets, and owls, and white-tailed deer sip the swamp's dark water.

Clouds reflect on the surface of the Combahee River, which flows through the wetlands of southern South Carolina near the Atlantic Coast.

Rivers and Lakes

Four large river systems, the Pee Dee, the Santee, the Edisto, and the Savannah, flow from the mountains to the Atlantic Ocean. Stretching 238 miles (383 kilometers), the Savannah is the longest.

South Carolina's largest lakes are all **reservoirs**. The dams that form these lakes provide electricity to the state's rural areas.

Climate

South Carolina has a warm, wet **climate**. This leads to sizzling hot summers and mild winters.

Hurricanes and other tropical storms strike South Carolina's coast about once every five to 10 years. In September 2017, Hurricane Irma brought strong winds, mighty waves, and floods.

MAXIMUM
TEMPERATURE
113°F

MINIMUM
TEMPERATURE
-19°F

During Hurricane Irma in 2017, winds blew at speeds of up to 72 miles (116 km) per hour in South Carolina.

Trees, Shrubs, and Flowers

South Carolina is home to many kinds of plants. Near the coast, oaks draped with Spanish moss stand beside palmettos and scrawny pines. In the Piedmont, dogwoods, oaks, and sugar maples are common. Bald cypress and tupelo gums grow in swampy areas. About 80 types of magnolias grow throughout the state. Meadows come alive with wildflowers, including purple coneflowers, sunflowers, Indian grass, and yellow jessamine, the state flower.

Spanish moss hangs from the branches of many oaks and other large trees in South Carolina.

From Bears to Birds

South Carolina has plenty of wildlife. The state animal, the white-tailed deer, lives in forests, swamps, and grasslands. Swamps and wetlands are home to alligators and 38 types of snakes. There are croaking toads and snapping turtles. Loggerhead sea turtles lay eggs on some South

In 1985, wood storks were nearly extinct. Today, there are thousands of nesting pairs in the wild. This species' survival is a South Carolina success story.

Carolina beaches. Black bears, raccoons, opossums, and salamanders roam the Piedmont. Red-tailed hawks and owls share the sky with tiny Carolina wrens, field sparrows, and noisy warblers. Wood ducks and geese swim in lakes and ponds. In wetlands, egrets and herons fish along the water's edge.

The dome on South Carolina's State House contains 44,000 pounds (19,958 kilograms) of copper.

CHAPTER 2

Government

When South Carolina was still a **colony**, it had just one major city: Charleston. Naturally, Charleston became the seat of the colonial government. When the United States formed, South Carolina needed a state capital. In 1790, Columbia officially took on the role. Work began on the capitol in 1855. Construction stopped in 1861 when the Civil War began, but the building was finally finished in 1903.

Three Branches

Patterned after the U.S. government, South Carolina's state government has three branches. The governor leads the executive branch, which carries out state laws. The legislative branch has a Senate and a House of Representatives. It makes state laws. The judicial branch interprets those laws. It is led by the state Supreme Court.

SOUTH CAROLINA'S STATE GOVERNMENT

JUDICIAL BRANCH
Enforces state laws

- Supreme Court
- Court of Appeals
- Trial Courts
  - Circuit Courts
  - Family Court
  - Probate Court
  - Magistrate Courts
  - Munic Cou
- Civil Court
- Court of Common Pleas
- Criminal Court

LEGISLATIVE BRANCH
Writes and passes state laws

- Senate (46 members)
- House of Representatives (124 members)

EXECUTIVE BRANCH
Carries out state laws

- Governor
- Lieutenant Governor

Department heads of:
Alcohol and Other Drug Abuse Services
Commerce
Corrections
Health and Human Services
Insurance
Juvenile Justice
and many more

Local governments provide protective services. Here, firefighters watch over a peace march in Charleston.

Counties and Cities

South Carolina is divided into 46 counties. Each has its own government. The head of a county government is called a manager. A county council makes laws about building, taxes, roads, and services. The state is also home to a total of 269 cities. Each city has a mayor and a city council. County and city governments hold regular meetings. They listen to citizens to determine what people want and do not want to happen where they live.

South Carolina's National Role

Each state elects officials to represent it in the U.S. Congress. Like every state, South Carolina has two senators. The U.S. House of Representatives relies on a state's population to determine its numbers. South Carolina has seven representatives in the House.

Every four years, states vote on the next U.S. president. Each state is granted a number of electoral votes based on its number of members of Congress. With two senators and seven representatives, South Carolina has nine electoral votes.

2 senators and 7 representatives

9 electoral votes

The average number of electoral votes per state is about 10. South Carolina is close to that number.

The People of South Carolina

Elected officials in South Carolina represent a population with a range of interests, lifestyles, and backgrounds.

Ethnicity (2016 estimates)

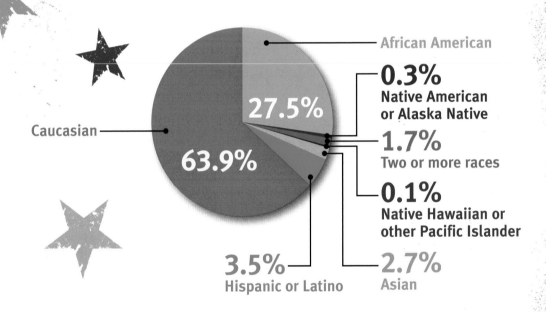

African American
27.5%

0.3%
Native American or Alaska Native

1.7%
Two or more races

0.1%
Native Hawaiian or other Pacific Islander

Caucasian
63.9%

3.5%
Hispanic or Latino

2.7%
Asian

85.6% of the population graduated from high school.

63.3% live in cities.

South Carolina is home to **368,959** veterans.

68.6% own their own homes.

4.8% of South Carolinians were born in other countries.

What Represents South Carolina?

States choose specific animals, plants, and objects to represent the values and characteristics of the land and its people. Find out why these symbols were chosen to represent South Carolina or discover surprising curiosities about them.

Flag

In 1775, Colonel William Moultrie designed South Carolina's state flag. Blue was the color of the Revolutionary War soldiers' uniforms. The crescent moon was the symbol on soldiers' caps. Forts built from palmetto trunks protected soldiers. It is said that cannonballs bounced off the tree's spongy trunks.

Seal

The state seal has two sides. It features both mottos of South Carolina. The mottos are in Latin. The one on the right means "While I breathe, I hope." The other means "Prepared in mind and resources." The seal was designed in 1777. A palmetto tree and the Roman goddess Spes (Hope) are also shown.

Yellow Jessamine

STATE FLOWER

This bright-yellow flower blooms on an evergreen vine that climbs trees and fences across the state.

Eastern Tiger Swallowtail

STATE BUTTERFLY

The hind wings of this lovely yellow-and-black butterfly look like the tail feathers of swallows.

Carolina Wren

STATE BIRD

Carolina wrens build their messy nests of grass in anything from flowerpots to old boots.

Sabal Palmetto

STATE TREE

Found along the coast, palmettos are also called cabbage palms or swamp cabbage.

Loggerhead Turtle

STATE REPTILE

Female loggerhead turtles return to the beach where they were born when it is time to lay their own eggs. They dig nests in the sand and lay about 100 eggs at a time.

Amethyst

STATE GEMSTONE

p-purple amethysts were found near e West, South Carolina. The largest es are displayed in the Smithsonian Institution in Washington, D.C.

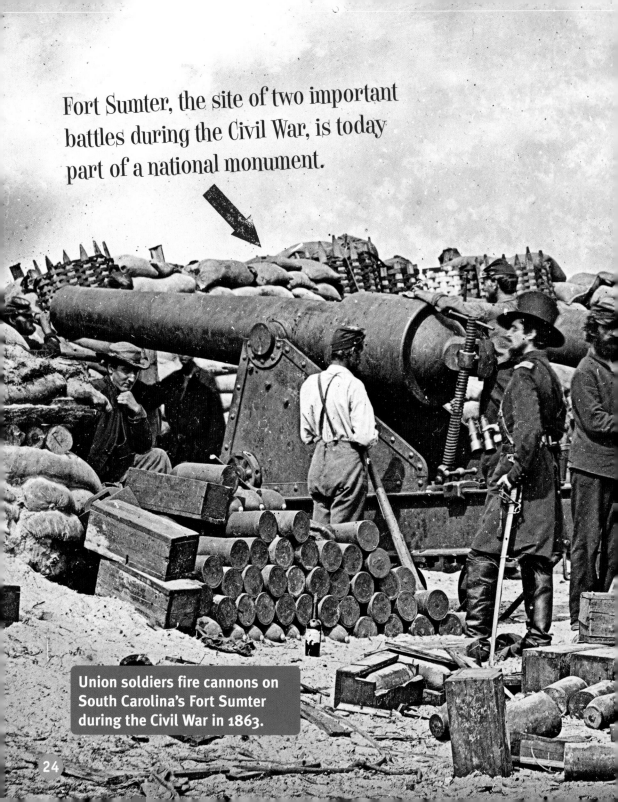

Fort Sumter, the site of two important battles during the Civil War, is today part of a national monument.

Union soldiers fire cannons on South Carolina's Fort Sumter during the Civil War in 1863.

History

South Carolina has changed a great deal over time. When Europeans first arrived in the region, they found a rich Native American culture. The area's Native Americans believed that no person could own land. The English disagreed. They formed a colony and took over the land to build farms, towns, and cities. Wealthy landowners grew rice, cotton, and indigo. Farming continues today, but South Carolina is changing. It has become a major shipping hub and a tourist magnet.

Native Americans from the Carolina region sometimes collected wild fruit as a source of food.

Native Americans

South Carolina's first residents were hunter-gatherers from more than 13,000 years ago. Early cultures hunted bison, mastodons, and mammoths for food. When those animals disappeared, so did the hunter-gatherers. New cultures took their place. People settled in villages. They traded shells, copper goods, handmade jewelry, and animal skins. They grew corn, beans, and squash. Those food crops fed villagers throughout the year.

At one time, more than 30 Native American groups settled the land. They traveled the rivers. They fished and clammed on the sandy shorelines. They hunted in the forests. Each group had its own traditions and occupied a different part of the state. The Cherokee lived in the mountains. The Cheraw, Wateree, Waccamaw, Santee, and Catawba peoples all spoke different versions of the Siouan language. Groups such as the Edisto lived along the coast.

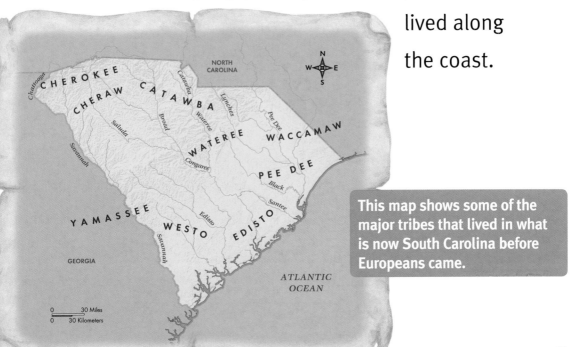

This map shows some of the major tribes that lived in what is now South Carolina before Europeans came.

The Spanish and the English

During the 1520s, Spanish explorers sailed into the region. The Spanish were the first Europeans to contact Carolina's native people. They captured and enslaved about 100 Native Americans. In 1526, 600 Spanish settlers tried to form a colony in the area. They brought African slaves with them. When the Spanish colony failed, the Africans stayed and joined local Native American tribes. These former slaves became the first people from abroad to live permanently in what is now the United States.

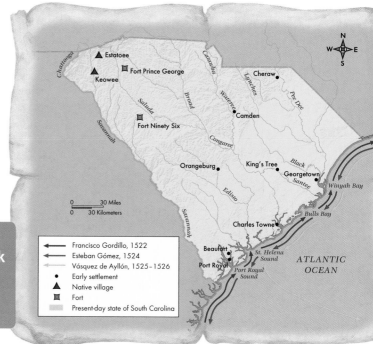

This map shows routes Europeans took as they explored and settled what is now South Carolina.

Carolina plantation owners grew wealthy from the hard work of slaves.

The French also tried to form a colony in what is now South Carolina. Captain Jean Ribault and his men built a fort in the region in 1562. Ribault returned to France for supplies and never came back. His men built their own ship and headed back to France.

In 1663, England founded a colony in the area and called it Carolina. Colonists were granted land to set up large **plantations**. Plantation owners bought slaves to work their fields. In 1712, Carolina was split into two separate colonies: North Carolina and South Carolina.

A New Nation

In 1774, South Carolina banded together with other British colonies to resist the British government. The following year, the Revolutionary War (1775–1783) started. When the war ended, the newly independent colonies decided to join together and form the United States of America. In 1788, South Carolina became the new country's eighth state.

Timeline of South Carolina Events

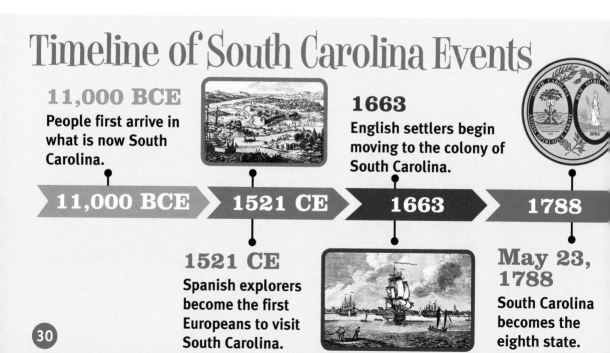

11,000 BCE
People first arrive in what is now South Carolina.

1663
English settlers begin moving to the colony of South Carolina.

11,000 BCE → 1521 CE → 1663 → 1788

1521 CE
Spanish explorers become the first Europeans to visit South Carolina.

May 23, 1788
South Carolina becomes the eighth state.

The Civil War

In the 1800s, South Carolina's **economy** relied on slave labor. Northern states began passing laws against slavery, but Southern states did not want to give up the practice. In 1860, South Carolina **seceded** from the United States and joined other Southern states to form a new nation. In 1861, its troops fired on Northern soldiers in Fort Sumter, beginning the Civil War (1861–1865). War swept across the South.

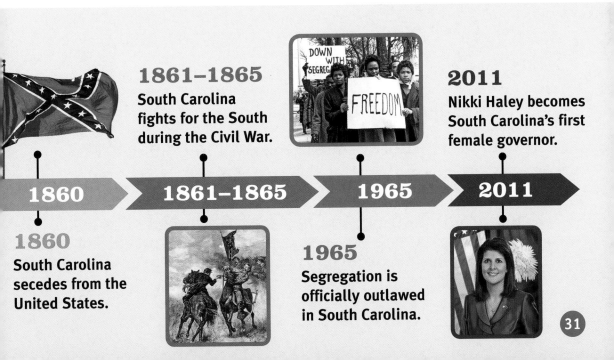

1861–1865
South Carolina fights for the South during the Civil War.

2011
Nikki Haley becomes South Carolina's first female governor.

| 1860 | 1861–1865 | 1965 | 2011 |

1860
South Carolina secedes from the United States.

1965
Segregation is officially outlawed in South Carolina.

Students at Claflin University in Orangeburg march in a civil rights demonstration in 1960.

Today's South Carolina

At the end of the war, slavery became illegal. However, South Carolina replaced it with **sharecropping**. The state passed laws to keep African Americans and whites **segregated**. In the early 1900s, many African Americans left South Carolina to find better jobs in factories in the North. In the 1960s, the state's African Americans protested for civil rights. Slowly, they began winning equal treatment. South Carolina **integrated** schools, restaurants, and other public places.

Mary McLeod Bethune

Mary McLeod Bethune (1875–1955) was a teacher and a civil rights activist. Often called the first lady of the struggle, she fought to improve education for African American children. Born in Mayesville, she was one of 17 children. She studied to be a teacher, married, and moved to Daytona Beach, Florida. There, she started the Daytona Educational and Industrial School for Negro Girls. It is known today as Bethune-Cookman University. In addition to her work as an educator, Bethune was also active in politics. She campaigned for President Franklin D. Roosevelt and was a close adviser during his time in office.

Each year, the Spoleto Festival brings 17 days of live music, theater, and dance performances to Charleston.

CHAPTER 4

Culture

South Carolina is all about southern hospitality. A visit to downtown Charleston or a historic plantation is like taking a step back in time. People at the beach dance the Shag, South Carolina's state dance. A visit to the Catawba Cultural Center in Rock Hill offers a glimpse into the state's Native American heritage. The culture is uniquely South Carolina, and the welcome mat is always out.

Sports and Recreation

College football is big in South Carolina. Thanksgiving is time for the Clemson–South Carolina football game. Every South Carolinian chooses a side in the annual face-off. Bragging rights for a year are at stake.

South Carolina has more than 450 golf courses. NASCAR drivers rev up their engines for the Bojangles' Southern 500 at Darlington Raceway.

South Carolina football fans anticipate the big face-off between the Clemson Tigers and the South Carolina Gamecocks each November.

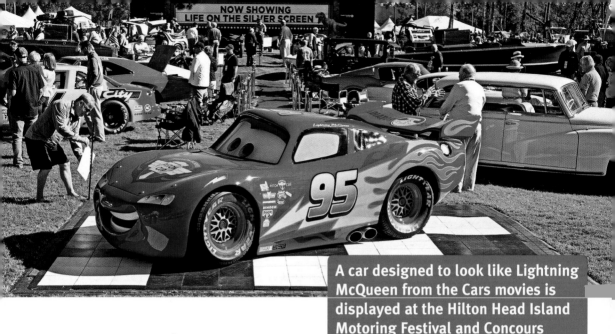

A car designed to look like Lightning McQueen from the Cars movies is displayed at the Hilton Head Island Motoring Festival and Concours d'Elegance.

Time to Celebrate

There are plenty of fairs and festivals in South Carolina. The state fair is held each year in Columbia. It offers amusement rides, funnel cakes, livestock competitions, and music. Some events, such as the Spoleto Festival, draw visitors from around the world. Others are less well-known but still interesting. The Sweet Grass Cultural Arts Festival in Mount Pleasant celebrates basketmaking. Car lovers flock to the Hilton Head Island Motoring Festival and Concours d'Elegance.

Each year, South Carolina workers pull in millions of pounds of shrimp from the state's coastal waters.

At Work

South Carolina's textile mills once produced miles of cotton thread and fabric. Today, the state has new business interests. For example, the state makes medicines and many plastic products. There are 25,200 farms spread across South Carolina, growing peaches, watermelons, cotton, and other crops. South Carolina's farmers also raise chickens, turkeys, and cattle. Fishers on the coast haul in crabs, clams, and other seafood.

Deep Orange 5 was designed by CU-ICAR students to appeal to people living in crowded cities where there is little space for parking.

CU-ICAR

Automobile manufacturing is big business in South Carolina. Many South Carolina students are also preparing to design the cars of the future. In 2007, the Clemson University International Center for Automotive Research (CU-ICAR) opened. The research center has about 200 students. They learn how to engineer cars and trucks. The students in this competitive program are studying for advanced degrees. When they graduate, they will work as automotive engineers. They will design cars and trucks for companies around the world.

Yum!

South Carolina has a rich tradition of southern cuisine. The state grows peaches, watermelons, collards, okra, and muscadine grapes. Favorite local dishes use collard greens, okra, and black-eyed peas. Roadside stands sell boiled peanuts, the official state snack. In Columbia, a popular meal is barbecue, coleslaw, and banana pudding.

Cheesy Grits

Ask an adult to help you!

Grits (ground, dried corn) are a daily part of South Carolina breakfasts, but you can enjoy them any time of day!

Ingredients
3 cups chicken broth
1 cup quick-cooking grits, uncooked
$\frac{1}{2}$ teaspoon salt
Pepper, to taste
1 tablespoon butter
2 cups shredded cheddar cheese

Directions
In a saucepan, bring the chicken broth to a boil over high heat. Stir in the grits, reduce heat to medium, and cook for six minutes. Add the salt, pepper, butter, and cheese. Stir until smooth. Serve hot and enjoy!

Greenville's Liberty Bridge spans 345 feet (105 meters) across the scenic Falls Park on the Reedy.

A Southern Star

South Carolinians enjoy making visitors feel welcome in their state. Residents and visitors alike love hiking mountain trails in the morning. They feast on fresh-caught shrimp and other local seafood specialties on the coast. They take in the rich history of Charleston. South Carolina remembers its history. It also welcomes new ideas and new people. This makes it the perfect place to live or visit! ⭐

Famous People

Edward Rutledge

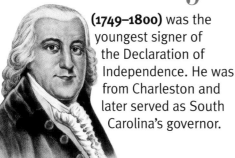

(1749–1800) was the youngest signer of the Declaration of Independence. He was from Charleston and later served as South Carolina's governor.

Andrew Jackson

(1767–1845) fought in the Revolutionary War and the War of 1812 and served as president of the United States from 1829 to 1837. He was born in the Carolina Colony.

John C. Calhoun

(1782–1850) served as the U.S. Secretary of War from 1817 to 1825, the vice president of the United States from 1825 to 1832, and a U.S. senator from South Carolina from 1845 to 1850. He was from Abbeville.

"Shoeless" Joe Jackson

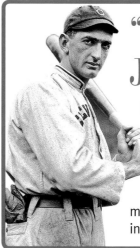

(1887–1951) played baseball for the Chicago White Sox. In 1919, his team lost the World Series. He and others were accused of losing on purpose to make money from a bet. He was born in Pickens County.

Peggy Parish

(1927–1988) was a children's book writer best known for her Amelia Bedelia series. She was from Manning.

James Brown

(1933–2006) was a musician who was called the godfather of soul. He was elected to the Rock and Roll Hall of Fame in 1986. He was born in Barnwell.

Jesse Jackson

(1941–) is a minister, activist, and politician who has long been a major figure in the fight for civil rights. He is from Greenville.

Mamie "Peanut" Johnson

(1935–2017) was the first woman to play as a pitcher in professional baseball's Negro Leagues. She was born in Ridgeway.

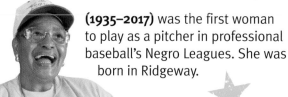

Stephen Colbert

(1964–) is a comedian and author best known for hosting the TV shows *The Colbert Report* and *The Late Show with Stephen Colbert*. He is from Charleston.

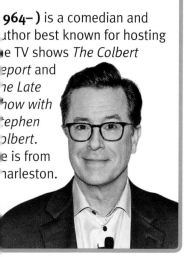

Viola Davis

(1965–) is one of the only actresses ever to win an Academy Award, an Emmy Award, and a Tony Award. She was born in St. Matthews.

Nikki Haley

(1972–) is a politician who became the first woman to serve as governor of South Carolina in 2011. She is from Bamberg.

Did You Know That . .

South Carolina is prone to earthquakes. The worst earthquake in South Carolina's history shook the state on August 31, 1886. There was no way to measure the power of an earthquake back then. However, more than 100 people died in the quake. Charleston's buildings suffered severe damage.

Eliza Pinckney, a plantation owner in colonial Charleston, developed a new cash crop for South Carolina. Pinckney grew and sold indigo. The plant was used to dye cloth blue. By 1747, indigo was South Carolina's second-best-paying crop.

The television show *Gullah Gullah Island* took place on South Carolina's St. Helena Island. The Gullah culture goes back to African slaves. The show used some Gullah language and traditions.

In 1773, the Charleston Library Society set up America's first museum. The museum is still in operation on Meeting Street in Charleston. Many of its exhibits deal with the Revolutionary War.

Georgia may be called the Peach State, but South Carolina actually grows more peaches. Peaches are such an important crop that the town of Gaffney has a water tower shaped like a giant peach.

Fort Sumter is in Charleston Harbor. On April 12, 1861, Confederate troops fired on the fort, igniting the Civil War. The fort is now a national monument.

Did you find the truth?

F English settlers were the first Europeans to visit South Carolina.

T South Carolina fought on the side of the South in the Civil War.

Resources

Books

Cunningham, Kevin. *The South Carolina Colony.* New York: Children's Press, 2011.

Ditchfield, Christin. *Exploring the South Carolina Colony.* Mankato, MN: Capstone Press, 2016.

Rozett, Louise (ed.). *Fast Facts About the 50 States: Plus Puerto Rico and Washington, D.C.* New York: Children's Press, 2010.

Somervill, Barbara A. *South Carolina.* New York: Children's Press, 2014.

Visit this Scholastic website for more information on South Carolina:
★ www.factsfornow.scholastic.com
Enter the keywords **South Carolina**

Important Words

climate (KLYE-mit) the weather typical of a place over a long period of time

colony (KAH-luh-nee) a community settled in a new land but with ties to another government

economy (i-KAH-nuh-mee) the system of buying, selling, making things, and managing money in a place

integrated (IN-tuh-gray-tid) included people of all races

piedmont (PEED-mahnt) lying or formed at the base of mountains

plantations (plan-TAY-shuhnz) large farms that produce crops such as cotton, coffee, sugar, and tea

plateau (pla-TOH) an area of level ground that is higher than the surrounding area

reservoirs (REZ-ur-vwahrz) artificial lakes in which water is collected and stored for use

seceded (si-SEED-id) formally withdrew from a group or an organization, often to form another organization

segregated (SEG-ruh-gay-tid) kept separate from the main group

sharecropping (SHAIR-krahp-ing) a system where a farmer works land owned by someone else and pays rent either in cash or in shares of crops grown

Index

Page numbers in **bold** indicate illustrations.

About the Author

Barbara Somervill has written more than 250 books on many different topics. She was born and educated in New York but now lives in South Carolina. She earned a degree in library science from the University of South Carolina. She loves to travel, read, and color!